Dream Interpretation Journal

 **TORN CURTAIN PUBLISHING**
Wellington, New Zealand
www.torncurtainpublishing.com

ISBN Softcover 978-1-991299-00-0
ISBN Epub 978-1-991299-01-7

All scripture is taken from the New American Standard Bible®, Copyright © 1960, 1971, 1977, 1995, 2020 by The Lockman Foundation. Used by permission. All rights reserved. lockman.org

Cataloging in Publishing Data
  Title: Dream Interpretation Journal
  Author: Amber N. Johnson, M.D.
  Subjects: Christian living; dream interpretation; prophetic dreams; body, mind & spirit; biblical studies; spiritual warfare; spiritual growth.

Dream Interpretation Journal

Deciphering What God is Speaking Through Our Dreams

Amber N. Johnson, M.D.

Contents

Introduction

"And it shall be in the last days," God says, "that I will pour out my Spirit on all mankind; and your sons and your daughters will prophesy, and your young men will see visions, and your old men will have dreams."
Acts 2:17

I love the language of dreams. Dreams are one of the most beautiful and intimate ways God communicates with us. With our conscious minds out of the way God can speak with us heart-to-heart, unhindered, and show us things that we may be too distracted—or reluctant—to talk about with Him when we are awake.

God has imparted so much to me through dreams—instruction and warning, deliverance and breakthrough, inner healing . . . and future-prophetic insight. In dreams, He has given me information and revelation that I may not have been as receptive to during my waking hours; for example, a prophetic word or promise for the future that my conscious mind did not yet have the faith for. God certainly may have been communicating the same message to me during the day, but my mind may have resisted that word from Him. In a dream, however, God can enlarge my awareness, increase my vision, show me the expansiveness of His heart for me, and reveal what is possible by His grace.

I've also had many dreams where the Lord started conversations aimed at healing me in ways I did not know I needed. It's very likely He had tried to speak with me about these things during waking hours too, but my subconscious response probably went something like, "Oh, no Lord, I'm fine! I'm totally over it. It doesn't bother me anymore!" Meanwhile, God was thinking, "Umm ... but you're actually not okay. There is still a part of your heart that is hurting." Healing happens in layers, and the fact that there are more layers to work through does not negate any healing that has already happened. The Lord wants us to experience full healing, and often it takes a dream for us to be willing to go all the way with Him.

In addition to revelation, dreams can also be a means of powerful encounter. These types of dreams don't need much in the way of interpretation because they are meant to be an encounter in and of themselves. Certain types of healing dreams work this way—after these dreams we wake up knowing that something has been released and we are healed! There are also *impartation dreams,* where God imparts spiritual gifts and anointing. And there are *warfare dreams,* where God teaches us to engage in spiritual warfare.

I absolutely love my dream communication with God! Everybody's dream language is unique and personal. The specific symbols God uses with me are different from those He uses with other dreamer friends of mine. Each of us have a unique relationship with God, and the uniqueness of these relationships will be reflected in our dream lives too. For all of us though, dreams bring a deeper dimension to relationship!

My relationship with God has significantly deepened through my dreams, and now I feel sad if I wake up without having had one! If I don't dream, it is usually an indicator that I am sleep-deprived. Recently, I went two or three nights in a row without a dream, which is quite unusual for me. I asked the Lord about it because I really missed meeting with Him that way. He told me that I wasn't remembering my dreams because I was too stressed. The following night, after repenting and surrendering my worries to Him, I had some of the most significant and impactful dreams of my life.

I honestly don't think I can put into words what a difference dreams make in my intimacy and relationship with God. It is like having Him speak a poem over me—one that has been written for my ears alone, with a meaning and intimacy intended for me and no one else. It truly is heart-to-heart communication. It is His 'deep' calling out to mine (Psalm 42:7) while I sleep.

I love to spend hours in the secret place with God. I enjoy His presence in corporate worship and feel His anointing when I give a weighty prophetic word. But while I love encountering Him in these ways, nothing will ever be able to match the love connection I've felt with God in my dreams.

Most of us spend one-third of our lives sleeping, and I have no doubt the Holy Spirit is determined to utilize that time! My prayer is that this dream journal will jumpstart your own journey with the Lord. I encourage you to dive in and discover the kisses from heaven that are waiting for you in your dreams.

PART ONE

"We have had a dream, and there is no one to interpret it."
Then Joseph said to them, "Do interpretations not belong to
God? Tell it to me, please."
Genesis 40:8

1

Interpreting Your Dreams

In 1 Corinthians 12:10 the Apostle Paul lists the interpretation of tongues as a gift of the Holy Spirit. Similarly, the interpretation of dreams, visions and prophetic symbols are from the Holy Spirit. In the words of Joseph to the butler and baker in Pharaoh's prison, "Interpretations belong to God" (Genesis 40:8).

This is important to remember because typically we want to search for the quick answer and leave the Holy Spirit out. I have a funny saying, but I use it because it tends to stick with people. "Interpretation is a gift of the Spirit, not a gift of Google!" In other words, Google does not know what the Holy Spirit is saying to you. Google might give an interpretation based on common sense and New Age symbols, but it can't give you the Holy Spirit's interpretation. As a rule, Google is off-limits when it comes to dream interpretation. An exception would be if the Holy Spirit directs a person to look up a specific detail such as a historical person, a place, or a name they need to know the meaning of in order to interpret the rest of the dream. Googling those types of things is okay, but only if the Holy Spirit directs you to look up those specific things. General googling and 'reflex googling' are banned!

Since interpretation is from God, there is no cookie-cutter formula to dream interpretation. My goal is to give you processes and tools to help you partner with the Holy Spirit as you press into what He is trying to tell you through your dreams. Ultimately, hearing from the Holy Spirit is the main thing. He is the dream interpreter! We can't come up with a dream interpretation through processes and protocols that omit listening to the Holy Spirit. Processes and tools are simply meant to aid us in learning how to listen to the Holy Spirit. The writer of the book of Hebrews understood this. In Hebrews 5:14 we read that we need to be trained in discernment. Similarly, dream interpretation takes practice.

I love the passage of Scripture where God teaches Jeremiah how to interpret prophetic visions. The Lord says, "What do you see, Jeremiah?" In turn, Jeremiah replies, "I see a branch of an almond tree" (Jeremiah 1:11). Then the Lord gives the interpretation:

> Then the Lord said to me, "You have seen well, for I am
> watching over My word to perform it."
> Jeremiah 1:12

To understand the symbolism of the dream, we need to look at the Hebrew words God uses. In Hebrew, the word for 'almond' is *saqed* and the word for 'watch over' is *soqed*. The words have completely different meanings, but in Hebrew, they sound very similar. They are soundalikes, in other words, a pun! God was using a wordplay to convey His message to the prophet.

Because the language of dreams is symbolic, God uses soundalikes, puns or symbols that mean something specific based on our personal experience and history with Him. Dream language is also poetic; it is meant to speak to each of our hearts in a way that the language of normal conversation doesn't quite reach. My dream language with

God is intimate and personalized to me, therefore the symbolism God uses in my dreams may very well differ from the symbolism He uses with anyone else on earth. Likewise, your dream language with God will be intimate and personalized to you. This is why we need the Lord to tutor us in dream interpretation, just as He taught Jeremiah how to interpret his prophetic visions.

Dream interpretation is a sub-category of prophetic interpretation, much like the analysis of prophetic words and visions. Whether we are seeking to understand a dream, vision or word, prophetic processing involves the same three components: *revelation, interpretation, and application.* In the case of dreams, the revelation is the dream itself. That's the easy part! But having a dream is only step one. We next need to ask the Holy Spirit for His help to interpret (or analyze) the dream and to apply it to our lives. In other words, we need Him to show us what it means and how we should respond to it.

But does everyone who experiences a God-dream also have the ability to interpret those dreams? Thankfully, the answer is that all of us can learn to interpret prophetic dreams. The apostle Paul wrote that the various kinds of gifts are from the same Holy Spirit (1 Corinthians 12:4) and advised the early church to "earnestly desire" the spiritual gifts, especially the gift of prophecy (1 Corinthians 14:1). James also encouraged the believers that if they lacked wisdom, they could ask God and He would generously give them wisdom (James 1:5). Similarly, Jesus made it clear that our Father in heaven readily gives good gifts to those who ask (Matthew 7:11).

Like spiritual gifts and heavenly wisdom, dream interpretation comes from God (Genesis 40:8). So, just as He gives us wisdom when we ask for it, God can help us interpret our dreams when we ask Him. Remember, the Holy Spirit is the dream interpreter—and He is readily available to give us the ability to interpret dreams when we ask for it because He lives inside us (1 Corinthians 6:19).

God gives us the gift or ability when we ask, but there is still a responsibility on our part to 'stir up' (or 'kindle afresh') our gifts (2 Timothy 1:6). We do this through practice! Spiritual gifts such as discernment, wisdom, knowledge, prophecy and healing require practice to mature. There are correct and incorrect ways to minister healing to people. It is the same when we give a word of wisdom or a word of prophecy. We need practice to discern both *what* God is saying and *why* He is saying it. God may give us a prophetic insight so we can share it, or to help us pray and intercede, or simply because we're His friends and He simply wants to tell us what is on His heart (Genesis 18:17). Dream interpretation is similar. It takes practice. I still have dreams that I don't fully understand. Often, it's only when the Holy Spirit gives me several dreams with the same theme that I start to get a better picture of what He is saying. It's a learning curve, and it's okay that it takes practice as we discover the ways He is wanting to speak to us. It's all part of the process of growing in intimacy.

Scripture promises that visions and dreams from God will increase in the end times (Acts 2:17). I very much believe that right now, God is pouring out dreams and visions on His church. He wants to connect with His people and share his heart with them through dreams and visions. If you are a person who dreams (science says you are!), then it is a given that God wants to communicate with you through dreams. So ask God for more dreams, and for the ability to interpret them through the power of the Holy Spirit!

2

Stewarding Your Dreams

It is a biblical principle that when we are faithful with what the Lord gives us, He is faithful to give us more (Matthew 25:14-30; Luke 16:10). How we steward our dreams is so important. Sometimes when I notice that I haven't had a dream for a few days, it's because I still haven't interpreted one from three days ago. It's as if the Lord is saying, "Why would I give you something new if you still haven't talked with Me about the last thing I said?" When I repent and sit with the Lord awhile, I soon receive the interpretation for my dreams. Usually I will have a new dream that same night.

Being a good steward of our dreams means not only that we seek the interpretation, but that we train ourselves to wake up and write the dream down. This requires self-control, especially if the dream comes in the early hours of the morning! It isn't easy to make the sacrifice of interrupted sleep, but it is always worth it to hear what the Lord is saying to us. People have different ways of recording dreams depending on what works best for them. Some people like to make a voice recording or use the speech-to-text function on their phones. My half-asleep voice at 3 a.m. sounds like mumbo-jumbo, so that doesn't work very well for me. Instead, I type out the dream in the Notes app on my phone (usually with a lot of sleepy typos, which I can correct in the morning). There are people who like to hand-write their dreams, and there are some who find they remember the dream better if they draw a picture rather than write it out in story form. Whatever method works for you is great, so long as you get it recorded! I will also add that waiting until morning rarely works. If you wake up from a dream in the middle of the night and then go back to sleep, there is a high chance you will not remember it in the morning.

My running record is eleven dreams in one night, and I will admit, I was a bit sleepy the day after! It is a sacrifice, but the Bible says that the one requirement of stewards is that they be found faithful (1 Corinthians 4:2). So, train yourself to wake up and record your dreams! Then spend intentional time with the Lord to let Him show you the interpretation. I promise you, the intimacy with Jesus is worth it!

What if I Don't Dream?

We all dream during our sleep. If you find yourself saying, "Not me . . . I don't have dreams," I encourage you to break that word curse in the name of Jesus and get to dreaming! I believe (and science agrees) that the issue isn't whether you dream, but whether you *remember* your dreams. So, ask the Holy Spirit for help.

When I was two and three years old, I often had nightmares. At the time I didn't know that these night terrors were demonic attacks, and it wasn't until much later in life that I learned how to take authority over them. And so, at a young age, I inadvertently partnered with a fear of dreams, which I believe is what shut off my ability to remember my dreams for many years. Eventually, I met some people who frequently had prophetic dreams. This stirred some sort of holy jealousy in me and I began praying, "God, I want to commune with You in this dream language!" I began asking for dreams and for help to remember them when I woke up.

The breakthrough came a number of years ago when I woke in the middle of the night feeling like I probably just had a dream or *should* have had one, but I didn't remember it. In that moment, something in me snapped—in a good way. I got up and proclaimed out loud over my bed, "In the name of Jesus, I am not getting back into this bed without having a dream tonight!" Then I got back into bed and had the first prophetic dream I could remember in years. The dream was incredibly symbolic, and I remember waking up and thinking, *I have no idea what this means!* Thus began a beautiful journey of learning to partner with the Holy Spirit to interpret my dreams, and since that moment I have dreamt almost every night—and often multiple times per night!

In addition to asking the Holy Spirit for help, another tip for remembering dreams is recognizing the need for self-control. When we wake from a dream, it takes self-control to stay awake and to write the dream down. If we wait until morning, we're more likely to forget the dream. We're also letting the Lord know that sleep is more important to us than listening to Him speak. To wake up properly in the night, however, requires training. It is a matter of submitting our will to Jesus and surrendering our very human need for sleep to Him. In that sense, it is similar to fasting. The human body needs food, but on occasion, we will surrender that need to the Lord in order to lean into closer intimacy with Him.

In the Bible, Paul wrote about the sacrifices he made to serve Christ, saying:

I have been in labor and hardship, through many sleepless nights, in hunger and thirst, often without food, in cold and exposure.
2 Corinthians 11:27

Just as we choose to go without food during a fast, when we receive a dream from the Lord we can choose to surrender the human need for sleep for the sake of pressing into the intimacy with the Lord that He is offering to us through the dream encounter. Waking up to write the dream down takes self-control, the surrender of our will and the sacrifice of interrupted sleep, but the unique intimacy that is available through the language of dreams is well worth the sacrifice.

3

The Source of Your Dreams

It is helpful to recognize that every dream has three main sources: they can be from God; they can be human in origin; or they can be demonic. Discerning the source of a dream requires the ability to distinguish spirits (1 Corinthians 12:10) which is a gift of the Holy Spirit. The same gift applies to any form of prophetic processing. When we receive a prophetic word from someone, the first step in processing that word is to ask the Holy Spirit to help us distinguish whether it is from the Holy Spirit, a demonic spirit, or a human spirit.

Let's start with demonic dreams, then we'll talk about human dreams, and finally, God-dreams.

Demonic Dreams

Demons are sneaky and often bring ideas to us in a way that makes us believe a thought is our own—not that it was presented by a demon. During the daytime, a demon might present a thought that says, "Nobody likes me." But if a demon were to come with the same agenda at night, it could present a dream in which everyone is speaking and acting in a way that makes you feel rejected. Since you are sleeping, the demonic suggestion comes in picture form rather than conscious thought form. Nightmares are an example of dreams that may come from demons. Nightmares can also be a manifestation of a fear you have in real life. Such fears may present through 'soul dreams' (which we will explore in the next section) but can also be exploited by the enemy to become more intense nightmares.

There are several ways to discern a demonic dream. The first is that they make us feel 'icky'. The second is that no instruction or new information is present in the dream. And thirdly, after the dream is over, we feel no call to action—unlike dreams that are meant to warn us or call us to intercession. For example, I recently dreamt that someone I knew was in a car accident, and in the dream I said, "Oh, I should have known to pray against this." This dream was not a nightmare; it was a call for me to intercede for this individual. The next morning, I canceled every assignment against this person to cause a car accident, and I pleaded the blood of Jesus over his car and his driving. I fully believe I prevented a would-be car accident through my intercession. In contrast, I once had a dream in which I was being attacked and bitten by bats. There was no call to action, no association to show me what these bats represented, and no ability to defend myself against them. It was just a 'bat attack', and I woke up with that icky feeling of having been dealt a demonic attack. That one was a straight-up nightmare, and I rebuked it!

If you suffer from frequent nightmares, I truly believe it is because the devil is trying to steal what God wants to speak to you in the night. Call that liar on his bluff! For those suffering from frequent or long-term nightmares, there may be some inner healing you need from past trauma. You may also need deliverance if a spirit of fear is messing with you for some reason. If you think either of these might be the case, I encourage you to seek help from someone who can minister inner healing and deliverance and help you get free from that fear.

As a believer, the devil has zero right to mess with you, waking or sleeping. But demons are criminals, so you do need to police the spiritual realm and enforce the rules. As you pursue what the Lord has for you in the land of dreams, I encourage you to pray Psalm ninety-one over your sleep. If you have struggled or are struggling with demonic attacks in the night, it is particularly powerful to read and declare verse five over yourself before you go to bed:

You will not be afraid of the terror by night, or of the arrow
that flies by day.
Psalm 91:5

And lastly, if you are still struggling, take communion at night and plead the blood of Jesus over your sleep. Communion is a powerful weapon of warfare!

Human (or Soul) Dreams

Human dreams come from one of two sources: from our bodies, and from our souls. Body (or physical) dreams can be induced by sleeping pills, medications, sickness, and pain in our bodies. If I have a dream that my arm is hurting or missing and then I wake up and find that I was sleeping in a weird position and my arm is asleep, there probably is no mysterious meaning behind the dream other than that my body wanted me to know my arm was being hurt.

Soul dreams, as the name suggests, are rooted in our mind, will, and emotion. If in my waking hours I have been worrying about an upcoming meeting or conversation, and then I have a dream in which I am worried about that upcoming meeting, this is likely a soul dream. My soul is trying to tell me that *Yup, I am still worried about this meeting even when I'm asleep.* Or maybe I have been hoping for something in real life, and in my dream I have that very thing! This is where it can get tricky—it is important to rely on the Holy Spirit for discernment when interpreting these kinds of dreams to distinguish whether this 'good thing' is from Him, or if it is simply from our own emotion and desire.

If we discern that a dream's source is our soul, it may not be necessary to dismiss the dream entirely. Sometimes soul dreams help reveal emotions that we may be burying during waking hours. Soul dreams can be great indicators of what is going on inside the deep parts of us, and as such, they can become conversation starters with the Lord that lead to healing and breakthrough. The conversation might start with, "Okay, Lord, I didn't realize how much I've been worrying about such-and-such, but it's showing up in my dreams so I must be more worried than I thought. I choose to surrender this situation to You. Can You help me rest, knowing You are taking care of it?"

As an aside, we should be aware that humans not only have a soul, but we have a spirit too. It is very important that we do not try to 'read' the spirit of another human when we give a prophetic word. We can accidentally do this by telling the person only what they want to hear and not what we fully discern for them. We want to make sure we give prophetic words that are insight from the Holy Spirit, not something we are picking up from the spirit of the person we are ministering to.

Psychics are people who give prophetic words that they receive from demons. Supernatural knowledge that comes from another source other than God is called divination, and God has very strong warnings against such activities (Deuteronomy 18:10-12). When we receive a word from a psychic, fortune teller, horoscope, or ouija board, we empower demons to carry out the word for us, which is never advisable! In contrast, when we receive a prophetic word from God, we empower angels on assignment to carry out the word, which is for our blessing!

God-Dreams

As believers, we should expect that the vast majority of our dreams will be God-dreams. This doesn't mean we won't ever have a soul dream, but I think that for us, God-dreams are more common. The wise King Solomon wrote, "It is the glory of God to conceal a matter, but the glory of kings is to search it out" (Proverbs 25:2). According to Revelation 1:6, we are kings, so this verse applies to us—we get the honor of searching out the hidden matters! God hides them *for us,* not *from us.* God loves to be sought out; He loves when we pursue Him in order to know His heart—and His thoughts toward us. God romances us in the language of dreams, and dream interpretation is how we romance Him in return.

It is important to note, however, that God-dreams often have pieces of soul mixed in. We don't want to dismiss an entire God-dream just because our soul spoke into part of it. For example, kisses for me generally represent covenant or impartation. I've kissed people in dreams that I would never kiss in real life. These God-dreams don't have any feelings of being sexual or romantic—I simply wake up knowing that God is asking me to impart a spiritual gift or calling to that person. Sometimes in these dreams, however, I'll kiss a person and then think, *Eww.* The kissing part is God symbolically telling me to impart something to that person, and the 'eww' part is my soul giving a commentary based on its black-and-white perception of the dream symbol. When I wake up and process the dream, I can clearly discern between what God is trying to say (impart such-and-such spiritual gift to this person) and my soul's commentary ("Eww, kissing"), which I need to ignore.

It is interesting to me that even unbelievers can have God-dreams. In Genesis 41:15, we read that Pharaoh had a dream that was meant to warn him and give him instruction on how to prepare for a coming famine. Abimelech had a warning dream too, telling him he better not touch Abraham's wife (Genesis 20:3). And Nebuchadnezzar had a future-prophetic dream about the kingdoms of the world and the coming dominion of Jesus (Daniel 2:1-46).

This brings us to the topic of weird dreams. Two of the three dreams I just mentioned contain particularly weird stuff: *sick corn eats fat corn, skinny cows eat fat cows; a giant multi-media statue gets hit by a heavenly boulder.* They're weird, and from God. People often dismiss all kinds of dreams as 'pizza dreams', by which they mean, "It must have been something I ate." I honestly think this is often our go-to reaction because dreams are usually symbolic, and when the meaning of a dream is not immediately apparent, people can be quick to dismiss it, thinking, *There's no way that means anything.* On the contrary! For me personally, the more I wake up saying, "What on earth was that?!" the more likely the dream is to completely rock my world and change the course of my life when I finally get the Holy Spirit's interpretation. Quite often, the more symbolic the dream, the more likely it is that I have had a God-dream and that I am on the verge of receiving the most beautiful kiss from heaven as I dive in to discover what the King has hidden inside that dream for me.

4

Types of God-Dreams

When we make our way through the numerous dreams recorded in the Bible, we can begin to categorize God's intention in speaking to us through dreams. Others have come up with many more categories than what I include here, so I have tried to narrow them somewhat because too many can be a bit overwhelming when we are trying to interpret a dream. I've also tried to make each category broad enough to cover things that the Lord may be saying through dreams that do not fit easily into any of these categories. In any case, we need to remember that since the Bible doesn't list outright the God-dream categories for us, we are certainly getting into anecdotal material, and that's okay.

Future-Prophetic and Revelatory Dreams

Personally, I think that prophetic dreams about the future are far less common than other types of God-dreams. We can generally expect to have a greater number of dreams that are instructive or aimed at our healing and wholeness than dreams that provide information about the future. It is helpful to think about this in terms of the percentage of time while we are awake that God spends telling us about the future versus the time He spends giving us instruction and wisdom or talking with us about the deep things in our hearts.

As a prophet, I receive a decent amount of future-prophetic information, however, way more of my time with the Lord involves learning my identity, learning about Him and the things on His heart, healing the deep parts of my heart, communing with Him, and receiving wisdom and instruction from Him. In fact, without all these other types of communication with the Lord, the future-prophetic information He gives me would probably decrease. Even so, in our dreams the Holy Spirit can and does tell us about things to come (John 16:13).

That being said, I have often been surprised when a dream that I thought was intended to bring healing or change my thinking, ended up being future-prophetic as what I saw in the dream later happened in real life! Those are the fun moments when I suddenly realize, "I dreamt this!" Quite often, I realize that I have left my 'dream analyzing session' thinking, *I am not getting the full interpretation here*, only to realize that I have tried to over-interpret something that was supposed to be taken more literally.

I have included revelatory dreams in the same broad category. These dreams are not prophetic in a future-prophetic sense, but because the revelation pertains to something that is happening now. I have woken from many dreams that revealed something that was happening right at that moment. I also once woke up from a dream prophesying, even though the dream itself didn't specifically contain future-prophetic information.

'Calling' Dreams

'Calling' dreams are a type of prophetic dream, but they deserve their own category. Plain and simple, a calling dream gives you information about your calling. I'll tell you about my calling dream as an example. In my dream, I was paralyzed and unable to speak. I was being pushed in a wheelchair by someone I couldn't see (I believe this represented the Holy Spirit) right up to the person who, at the time, I considered my spiritual leader. My spiritual leader spoke and called me a prophet. Immediately, I jumped out of the wheelchair. At that moment, I was completely healed in my dream and was able to speak and move again.

When I woke, I felt the presence of the Holy Spirit so powerfully. That dream was how I found out that I am called as a prophet. That word 'prophet' was so clear in the dream! I was deeply impacted by that incredible dream for months, if not years. Yet it was also uncomfortable for me. For months I tried to pretend that the person in the dream had said, "gift of prophecy". But I had heard the word 'prophet' and I knew it! I eventually had to have my moment with the Lord where I decided if I was going to accept the calling on my life as a prophet. My calling was later confirmed by other prophets and apostles, which is an important part of the proper protocol for confirming ministry-calling words.

I have also had other calling-related dreams such as those in which I am speaking to large audiences. These are future-prophetic, but also could arguably be placed in the 'calling' category, telling me I am called to preach. This is an example of how the dream categories can overlap a bit.

Wisdom and Instruction Dreams

Some dreams give us wisdom for problems we are facing or instruction from the Lord for something He wants us to do. This dream journal came out of such a dream. I dreamt that I was on a Zoom call with a lady, and on the call she was promoting her ministry materials. I was particularly intrigued by her dream interpretation journal. I somehow received the book out of the screen and started looking through the dream journal (rules of physics don't apply in dreamland). In the dream, I decided that I didn't want to buy this specific book from the lady, but that hearing about her dream interpretation ministry was intended to spark an idea in my mind to make a similar instructive dream journal as a helpful resource for the church to use in learning dream interpretation.

Three days later, I was on a Zoom call in real life, and at the end of the call, one of the ladies started promoting her ministry. She then talked about her work with dream interpretation. Because my dream was instructive, I knew that I was not to use this woman's resources directly but to let the conversation inspire me to write this journal that you now have in your hands. This is an example of a dream that was future-oriented in that it gave instruction for a circumstance three days in the future, but these types of dreams can also give wisdom and instruction for a current situation we are already seeking solutions for.

Healing Dreams

In my opinion, healing dreams probably make up a fairly large proportion of the dreams we receive from God. This is because God will continue to give us dreams that relate to an area of our hearts that needs healing until that thing gets healed. Inner healing often happens in layers as we go through a process involving repentance, the forgiveness of self and others, breaking agreement with lies and curses that have been spoken over us, surrendering our fleshly defense mechanisms, and renewing our minds with the truth of who Jesus says we are.

As an example, I recently had a dream in which I was invited to a fancy dinner where I was going to be promoted and recognized. I put on a fancy dress and got ready to go, but on the way I had to stop and talk to someone from my past who had abused me. I had no choice—I had to stop at his table and talk with him before I could move on to the fancy dinner. In the dream I was so embarrassed that I had to talk with him, and to be honest, I woke up from the dream a bit frustrated. I knew the Lord was telling me there was something about this situation from my past that I still was not healed from and that I needed to be healed from it before I could go on to my next promotion in the spirit.

The reason I was frustrated was that I felt like I had already dealt with this situation. I had been through an extensive inner healing session with my mentor, had broken shame off myself, and broken my agreement with many lies. I had also gone through multiple sessions with the Lord, delivering myself from the trauma. However, according to this dream, there was still another layer of healing to go.

I honestly sat with that dream for hours before I finally heard the Holy Spirit reveal the exact lie that was hindering my remaining healing. It was a word-curse that had been spoken over me by another woman in relation to the situation. The thing that had been spoken was so obviously false, and I didn't think I had come into agreement with it. However, I suddenly realized that some little part of my heart had received that lie and believed what she said about me. I cried healing tears as I repented for believing that lie, broke agreement with it, and then spoke the truth over myself. I received a significant level of healing that day, and I'm so glad the Lord refused to let up on this in my dreams until we finally got all the way to the very last lie that needed to be broken to release my full healing.

There are also times when the Lord heals you in the dream itself. My dream about going into the banquet was meant to be a conversation starter with the Lord so He could help me find the key to my remaining healing. Other types of dreams bring healing and breakthrough in and of themselves. When you wake up from this type of dream, your heart has shifted in a beautiful way, and you know something inside of you just got fixed. God will heal inner soul wounds as well as physical maladies through these types of healing dreams.

The example I like to share is a dream in which the Lord healed me from past church hurts by having my current pastor hug me in the dream. The events of the dream were so simple; no hours of interpretation were needed with that one because it wasn't meant to give me information or revelation that I needed to discern through interpretation. Instead, this dream was an encounter where the Lord healed my heart through the dream itself. I woke up and was not afraid to trust anymore. Something supernatural had happened in the dream—there is no other explanation! When I woke up I was suddenly unafraid and had a restored ability to trust.

These types of healing dreams don't require us to interpret them since the dream is meant to be an encounter. Instead, the best way to respond is to spend time meditating on the dream. I have had dreams that have healed such incredibly deep things in me. I very much believe that the Lord hides pieces of our healing inside other people and that there are aspects of our healing that He won't do outside of community because community and Kingdom relationships are just that important to Him. But I am also a believer in the power of one radical encounter with Jesus, where He can undo so much past hurt and bring so much wholeness in a moment.

After some of these moments in which the Lord has touched the particularly deep and vulnerable places in my heart, it is so good to make time to just sit with Him and meditate on His goodness and the healing that He is doing, allowing my mind and emotions to be renewed with the reality of what He has done for me.

Encouragement and Impartation Dreams

Encouragement dreams make you feel loved and supported by the Lord. They speak to how the Lord sees you and remind you of your identity in Him. Impartation dreams allow you to receive gifts or anointing of the Holy Spirit in the dream. Impartation dreams can sometimes involve a prophet, pastor or other spiritual leader showing up in your dream. The individual may call you out, promote you, or bless you. For example, a prophet might show up in a dream to impart the gift of prophecy to you, or a spiritual leader might show up to impart gifts of the Holy Spirit or the anointing of the Holy Spirit.

I have had dreams in which the Holy Spirit comes upon me with great power. One such dream was rather short, and mostly involved walking through an open door, but when I walked through the door, I was hit strongly with the power of the Holy Spirit. I have at times woken up from dreams like this speaking in tongues. I have also had dreams in which I go into various demon-infested places and cast out all the demons, and I've had dreams in which I raise people from the dead. I believe that in those dreams I was receiving anointings for deliverance and resurrection.

Warning and Correction Dreams

Warning dreams are dreams where the Lord wants to make us aware and warn us to stop doing something or to not do something we would have done. There are many examples of these in the Bible, including Abimelech receiving a warning through a dream to not touch Abraham's wife (Genesis 20:3), the wise men being warned through a dream to not return to Herod (Matthew 2:12), and Joseph receiving a warning in a dream to go to Egypt to escape from Herod (Matthew 2:13). I have known people who have had dreams like these in which God warned them that they were headed for an affair. One time after going through pain from a church experience, I had a dream that I missed a communication on my pager at work, and I knew the Lord was telling me I needed to quickly forgive or I would miss His next instructions.

Correction dreams are similar. While they may not have a warning of impending danger the way warning dreams do, they still reveal something that is not correct in the way we are thinking or behaving. Warning and correction dreams alike call us to repentance and to change our way of thinking or behaving.

Intercession Dreams

If a warning is intended for another person, then it is categorized as an intercession dream. In this case, your responsibility is to pray and intercede for that person. The dream I mentioned earlier about the car accident was an intercession dream. In the dream, a specific person was involved in a bad crash, and I responded by saying, "I should have known and could have prayed to stop it." I woke up knowing this was a call from the Lord to intercede for this individual and cancel every assignment of car accidents. The person doesn't need to know that I protected him from a car accident. Nor was it my job to tell him to drive carefully; all that would have done was create fear. Instead, my job was to intercede.

Warfare Dreams

Spiritual warfare dreams are different from nightmares because in warfare dreams, you win! You wake up with the attack over and done because you conquered something! This is different from a nightmare, where you wake up feeling gross or scared afterwards, with the feeling of being under demonic attack. I had a dream once where rats were running all over me. Rats are generally symbolic of a demonic attack for me. In the dream itself, I started saying, "Jesus, Jesus, Jesus," over and over. I woke up from the dream still speaking the name of Jesus. Rather than being simply a nightmare, the attack was broken in the dream itself. This was a warfare dream.

We can actually go through a process of training ourselves to do spiritual warfare in our dreams. It is just like facing a spiritual attack during the daytime, only you are training your spirit to do warfare at night too. In one such dream, I was approached by a witch. In the dream, I rebuked whatever she was trying to do and walked toward her with authority as she retreated from me. In the dream, I told her, "Go to your room until you are ready to be delivered." She complied and went upstairs to her room. I woke up knowing I had conquered the season of attack I had been in.

5

Processing Your Dreams

Processing a dream first involves getting it into a format that is ready for interpretation. Since I type my dreams into my phone, my process starts with printing my record of the dream, cutting it out, and taping it into my notebook. I tape it onto the left side of the notebook and leave the page on the right for the interpretation. I don't know anyone else who does it this way, but this is what I've found works for me. In whatever way you prefer, get the dream in a format that you can look at and take to the Lord as you get ready to interpret.

Also, be sure to date your dream. This is so helpful when you look back. Sometimes dreams are future-prophetic, and we might not realize it at the time until we see the dream happen in real life! It is fun to be able to look back and see how far ahead of time God gave us the prophetic insight. Dates can also be important for other types of dreams because, for example, healing dreams will be focused on whatever is needing to be healed in you at that time of your life.

After you have the dream formatted, dated and ready to go, you can begin interpreting! This is the process I recommend when interpreting dreams:

1. Pray and invite the Holy Spirit. The Holy Spirit is the interpreter, so step one is to invite Him into the process (Genesis 40:8). We won't get anywhere without Him, so this is the place to start!

2. Write down the general emotion or feel of the dream. This can be helpful as we process and ask the Holy Spirit what type of dream this is.

3. Write down the focus of the dream. This step is critical because the whole interpretation is centered around the focus of the dream. If you are a major participant in the dream, then you are the focus. Most of our dreams will be about us, so in a very high percentage of dreams, you will be the focus. There might be more than one focus and if so, you can write down more than one. It is also helpful to determine who is at the center of the dream. Then write down a few others who are present in the dream. Remember, focuses and sub-focuses don't have to be people. They might be animals, trees, buildings, or whatever is taking center stage in the dream.

    Some people find it helpful to map this out in picture form. For example, you can draw a circle with the word "me" inside it, indicating that you are the focus, and then draw other circles that are connected to the main one, and inside those smaller circles, you can write the sub-focuses (e.g. 'tree', 'hotel', 'Aunt Betty'). If you are not an active player but an observer in the dream and are watching the events unfold without playing an active role in them, then probably something or someone else besides you is the main focus.

4. Write down what role you are playing in the dream. This is related to step three and can help in completing that step. You can write that you are the 'main person' or an 'observer' or a 'sub-focus.'

5. Ask the Holy Spirit if this dream is from Him or from your soul (or from a demon, but hopefully we immediately just throw those away and move on!). Remember that dreams can have components of both. You may have a God-dream with bits of your soul thrown in, and that's okay. If you aren't sure, it's alright to move on to the next steps. It might become apparent along the way which parts are from Him, and which parts are from your soul piping in.

6. Ask the Holy Spirit what type of God-dream this is. This might be readily apparent; for example, if it is bringing up a sensitive issue from the past or there is symbolism in the dream suggesting you are sick, then there is a good chance it is a healing dream. Lots of dreams are not so obvious though. If the Holy Spirit doesn't seem to reveal the type of dream right away, that is okay. It will become apparent as you move on to the next steps, so it is okay to fill this step in whenever it becomes clear.

7. Now that you know what the focus is, ask the Holy Spirit, "What is happening to the main person in the dream story?" In this step, we are getting the big picture, and we might start to get a gist of the type of dream this is. Is the focus of the dream facing or overcoming a challenge, figuring a problem out, seeing something in a new way, or moving to a new place? The emotion of the dream can be helpful as well, as we process this with the Holy

Spirit. When dreams are super symbolic, it can be easy to get lost in the details which may or may not matter. Why is Uncle Bob randomly in one tiny piece of the dream? Is that important? Maybe, maybe not. Perhaps Uncle Bob represents something, or maybe your brain remembered some random thing associated with Uncle Bob and thought it would be a good idea for him to join this dream party. That part is for later. For now, ask the Holy Spirit what the overall gist is. What is the big picture of the things that are happening in this dream?

8. Once you have the overall gist, you can go back and ask the Holy Spirit about the details. Ask Him questions. *Is such-and-such significant?* (If not, maybe that is part of a soul-dream). The only way to know if the details and symbols are significant is to ask the Holy Spirit. If it seems He is highlighting something to you as an important symbol, ask Him what it means. This takes patience and listening skills. Remember, no googling! Google doesn't know. The Holy Spirit does. This isn't a race to figure it out the fastest. It's a journey in intimacy and friendship with the Holy Spirit. If He wanted to tell you flat out, then He would have! But He didn't. He is instead showing you piece by piece through a dream because He is inviting you to have a heart-to-heart connection with Him.

God is being intentional with you when He speaks through the beautiful, poetic language of dreams. So carve out time to listen to Him. May you enjoy diving into beautiful times of intimacy with the Lord while you discover the secrets He longs to reveal to you in your dreams.

Sample Dream Dictionary

Note: *This is my dream dictionary. I have included it as an example, but it is important to remember that many of these symbols will mean something entirely different to me than what they may mean to you. The Holy Spirit also reserves the right to change the meaning of a dream symbol from one dream to the next. He is after a relationship, not a formula, so you will need to create a dream dictionary of your own. That being said, I hope that the following examples will guide you in seeing how these dream symbols work, and how they can help to spark your own fun journey with the creativity of the Holy Spirit.*

People

It takes good listening to the Holy Spirit to get the correct interpretation about people. There are a few keys, however. Most of the time, if someone in our inner circle features in our dream, it probably represents the literal person—but not always. For example, in a dream my dad can be (1) literally my dad, (2) Father God, or (3) a spiritual father or pastor in my life. A person in a dream can also represent the emotion or feeling I have toward that person. There is one person from my past who I always felt confused around, and he has represented confusion in some of my dreams. Sometimes the person might also represent the meaning of the person's name (e.g. Victoria represents victory etc.). Interestingly, children in my dreams generally mean specific people I'm called to minister to, often including healing for childhood wounds and trauma.

Animals

For me personally, snakes, rats, bats, spiders, beetles and bees represent demonic attacks. Snakes can denote deception due to their association with the snake in the Garden of Eden. Spiders and bats tend to be associated with the occult or witchcraft. Puppies in my dreams often represent either nonspecific people I'm ministering to (caring for puppies gives me a general ministry context in dreams) or people God is giving me compassion for (because puppies melt my heart, I guess). Animals can have different meanings for different people though; someone who is afraid of dogs might find that dogs represent something negative like fear or an attack. In my dreams, bears represent judgment (from the story in 2 Kings 2:24) and eagles represent the prophetic, or prophetic vision.

Numbers

The Bible is full of numbers and God often speaks through numbers. The numbers 3 and 7 are commonly recognized as having biblical significance but there are lots of symbolic numbers in Scripture. For example, there are 12 tribes of Israel, 12 apostles, and 12 foundation layers to New Jerusalem—the number 12 seems to be associated with the government of God's Kingdom throughout Scripture. It is important to be aware that the enemy uses counterfeits, and there are New Age meanings for numbers too, so I caution against using websites that have any kind of New Age feel or association. I trust and recommend Troy Brewer's book *Numbers that Preach,* as well as his website and YouTube videos (Troy Brewer Ministries). He bases his interpretation of numbers on the Bible and is well-studied in the Bible's use of numbers.

Here are some numbers that come up regularly for me personally with a consistent meaning: **2** refers to a double portion; 3 is about establishing something or completion; **5** is grace; **7** is the Spirit; **8** is new beginning; **10** is God's perfect order; **11** is prophet, transition, or God's stamping His approval on something; **12** is apostle or the government of the Kingdom; **13** is rebellion; **14** is double portion; **17** is victory; **22** is Kingdom keys (Isaiah 22:22); **30** is start of ministry (Luke 3:23); **40** is end of wilderness (Deuteronomy 29:5); **50** is Jubilee (Leviticus 25:11-13)

These are not absolute, though! For example, instead of victory, 17 could mean Psalm 17 or Proverbs 1:7. I went through a season recently where I was seeing the number 23 everywhere and the Lord was highlighting Psalm 23 to me. Numbers can have different meanings from one dream to the next, so it is important to ask the Holy Spirit. He might say, "Look up Troy Brewer" or He might say, "It's a psalm."

Colors

Like numbers, colors have meaning in the Bible. Colors can also have a wide variety of meaning based on your history and feelings about certain colors. For example, I have had so many positive dreams with the color green indicating I have a green light and green means 'go', but I have also had green in association with witchcraft (in one dream there was a green haze around a store and I knew it represented witchcraft). Witchcraft isn't exclusively green for me though, because I've also had witchcraft represented by purple fire. But purple isn't always bad for me either; purple can also mean royalty or wealth as with Lydia (Acts 16:14). Red can represent redemption or the blood of Jesus, but depending on the context it could also mean anger. Yellow is often associated with hope or joy. Blue can represent peace, sadness, or a priestly call (Exodus 28:31). White can mean clean and pure, or it can mean the spirit of religion, depending on the context. The context matters in determining if a color has a positive or negative meaning, and if a color is one you don't like or one you associate with something specific, it might mean something entirely else for you! Colors are not always important, but if a color seems to be highlighted in a dream or stands out as important then it is worth asking the Holy Spirit if it has a particular meaning.

Other dream symbols

Symbol	Meaning
Airport or airplane	Taking off in my calling or going to a new level in the Spirit
Bathroom	Cleansing, getting rid of the junk
Bedroom	Place of intimacy, privacy
Car	Calling
Car crashing	Person living life recklessly outside the Lord's will or leading, crashing their calling
Changing clothes	New identity, stepping into identity
Ears clogged	Not hearing what the Lord is trying to say
Edamame	Separation. This one still makes me laugh and it's a good example of how the Holy Spirit sometimes uses funny symbolism to get a point across. The Lord had been encouraging me in my waking hours to create space from a particular person. I kept having dreams about needing edamame, and finally, 'truckloads of edamame'.

	Interpretation hit suddenly: Just as you have to separate the pod to get the edamame bean out, I needed 'truckloads' of separation from this person!
Elevator (Going up)	Going up in the spirit or to new levels in the spirit
Elevator (Going down)	Dealing with deep issues
Food	Provision, sustenance, or possibly spiritual food
Gas station	Fill up with the Spirit (oil represents the Holy Spirit)
Hair	Anointing (Judges 16:17)
High heels	Healing, my anointing
Hotel	Place or season of transition
Kiss	Covenant, impartation
Laptop	Revelation/Holy Spirit insight
Liver disease	Effects of the sin of adultery (Proverbs 7:23)
Nakedness	Feeling exposed, shame, or vulnerable
Old house	Past issues, talking about something in the past
Pager going off	God trying to get my attention
Phone	Connection with God, or means of talking to God

Pregnancy or giving birth	Pregnant with, or birthing something in the spirit, birthing a ministry or revival or new spiritual level or spiritual breakthrough
School or classroom	Time of learning, God teaching me something
Shoes	Path, calling, or walking in Kingdom assignment
Showering	Cleansing
Submarine	Hidden issues, something lurking under the surface
Suitcase	Transition, going into a new season
Swimsuit or swimming pool	Immersion in the Spirit, baptism in the Holy Spirit
Teeth	Wisdom
Test	God testing me, time of testing
Train	Move of God
Television or movie	Prophetic vision, prophetic destiny

List of Dreams in the Bible

1. **Abimelech's Warning (Genesis 20:3)**

   Category: Warning

2. **Jacob's Ladder (Genesis 28:12-15)**

   Category I: Prophetic (Descendants will be multiplied v.14, also prophetic about Jesus, see John 1:51)

   Category II: Encouraging/comforting (God says He will be with him and keep His promises to him, v.15)

3. **Jacob to Return Home (Genesis 31:10-13)**

   Category: Instruction

4. **Laban's Warning (Genesis 31:24)**

   Category: Warning

5. **Joseph's Grain (Genesis 37:5-8)**

   Category: Prophetic

6. **Joseph's Sun, Moon, and Stars (Genesis 37:9-11)**

   Category: Prophetic

7. **The Cupbearer (Genesis 40:9-15)**

   Category: Prophetic

8. **The Baker (Genesis 40:16-19)**

    Category: Prophetic

9. **Pharaoh's Cows (Genesis 41:1-37)**

    Category: Prophetic

    Of note, Joseph interprets and then receives wisdom from God to apply the interpretation (see Genesis 41:33-36 in which Joseph advises to save one-fifth of the grain in the plenteous years to provide for the famine years). Every prophetic revelation, whether dream, prophecy or vision, needs (1) revelation, (2) interpretation, and (3) application.

10. **Pharaoh's Grain (Genesis 41:1-37)**

    Category: Prophetic

11. **Barley Loaf in Midian Camp (Judges 7:13-15)**

    Category: Encouragement

12. **Solomon (1 Kings 3:5-15)**

    Category: Impartation (Solomon receives an impartation of wisdom)

13. **Nebuchadnezzar's Statue (Daniel 2:1-45)**

    Category: Prophetic

14. **Nebuchadnezzar's Tree (Daniel 4:4-27)**

    Category: Warning (since Nebuchadnezzar didn't heed the application stated in verse 27 to repent, the dream could also be categorized as prophetic because it came to pass. *See Daniel 4:28-37.* If he had heeded the warning, it would have not come to pass).

15. **Daniel's Beasts (Daniel 7:1-28)**

   Category: Prophetic

16. **Joseph to Marry Mary (Matthew 1:20-25)**

   Category: Instruction

17. **Wise Men (Matthew 2:12)**

   Category: Warning

18. **Joseph's Warning about Herod (Matthew 2:13-15)**

   Category I: Warning

   Category II: Instruction (to go to Egypt)

19. **Joseph to Return from Egypt (Matthew 2:19-20)**

   Category: Instruction

20. **Joseph's Warning to Avoid Judea (Matthew 2:22)**

   Category: Warning

21. **Pilate's Wife (Matthew 27:19)**

   Category: Warning

22. **Paul's Dream of the Macedonian Man (Acts 16:9-10)**

   Category: Instruction

PART TWO

My Dream Dictionary

Symbol	Meaning

Symbol	Meaning

Symbol	Meaning

My Dream Journal

Date: _____ God Dream ☐   Soul Dream ☐

Emotion: _____

Category: _____

Focus(es): _____

Sub-focuses: _____

Dream: _____

_____

_____

_____

_____

_____

_____

_____

_____

_____

_____

_____

_____

_____

_____

_____

_____

_____

Interpretation:

Date: _____ God Dream ☐   Soul Dream ☐

Emotion: _____

Category: _____

Focus(es): _____

Sub-focuses: _____

Dream: _____

_____

_____

_____

_____

_____

_____

_____

_____

_____

_____

_____

_____

_____

_____

_____

_____

_____

Interpretation:

Date: _____ God Dream ☐   Soul Dream ☐

Emotion: _____

Category: _____

Focus(es): _____

Sub-focuses: _____

Dream: _____

_____

_____

_____

_____

_____

_____

_____

_____

_____

_____

_____

_____

_____

_____

_____

_____

_____

Interpretation:

Date: _____ God Dream ☐ Soul Dream ☐

Emotion: _____

Category: _____

Focus(es): _____

Sub-focuses: _____

Dream: _____

_____

_____

_____

_____

_____

_____

_____

_____

_____

_____

_____

_____

_____

_____

_____

_____

_____

Interpretation:

Date: _____ God Dream ☐   Soul Dream ☐

Emotion: _____

Category: _____

Focus(es): _____

Sub-focuses: _____

Dream: _____

_____

_____

_____

_____

_____

_____

_____

_____

_____

_____

_____

_____

_____

_____

_____

_____

_____

Interpretation:

Date: _____ God Dream ☐ Soul Dream ☐

Emotion: _____

Category: _____

Focus(es): _____

Sub-focuses: _____

Dream: _____

_____

_____

_____

_____

_____

_____

_____

_____

_____

_____

_____

_____

_____

_____

_____

_____

_____

Interpretation:

Date: _____ God Dream ☐   Soul Dream ☐

Emotion: _____

Category: _____

Focus(es): _____

Sub-focuses: _____

Dream: _____

_____

_____

_____

_____

_____

_____

_____

_____

_____

_____

_____

_____

_____

_____

_____

_____

_____

_____

_____

Interpretation:

Date: _____ God Dream ☐   Soul Dream ☐

Emotion: _____

Category: _____

Focus(es): _____

Sub-focuses: _____

Dream: _____

_____

_____

_____

_____

_____

_____

_____

_____

_____

_____

_____

_____

_____

_____

_____

_____

Interpretation:

Date: _____   God Dream ☐   Soul Dream ☐

Emotion: _____

Category: _____

Focus(es): _____

Sub-focuses: _____

Dream: _____

_____

_____

_____

_____

_____

_____

_____

_____

_____

_____

_____

_____

_____

_____

_____

_____

_____

Interpretation:

Date: _____ God Dream ☐   Soul Dream ☐

Emotion: _____

Category: _____

Focus(es): _____

Sub-focuses: _____

Dream: _____

_____

_____

_____

_____

_____

_____

_____

_____

_____

_____

_____

_____

_____

_____

_____

_____

_____

_____

Interpretation:

Date: _____ God Dream ☐   Soul Dream ☐

Emotion: _____

Category: _____

Focus(es): _____

Sub-focuses: _____

Dream: _____

_____

_____

_____

_____

_____

_____

_____

_____

_____

_____

_____

_____

_____

_____

_____

_____

_____

Interpretation:

Date: _____ God Dream ☐   Soul Dream ☐

Emotion: _____

Category: _____

Focus(es): _____

Sub-focuses: _____

Dream: _____

_____

_____

_____

_____

_____

_____

_____

_____

_____

_____

_____

_____

_____

_____

_____

_____

_____

Interpretation:

Date: _____ God Dream ☐   Soul Dream ☐

Emotion: _____

Category: _____

Focus(es): _____

Sub-focuses: _____

Dream: _____

_____

_____

_____

_____

_____

_____

_____

_____

_____

_____

_____

_____

_____

_____

_____

_____

_____

Interpretation:

Date: _____ God Dream ☐   Soul Dream ☐

Emotion: _____

Category: _____

Focus(es): _____

Sub-focuses: _____

Dream: _____

_____

_____

_____

_____

_____

_____

_____

_____

_____

_____

_____

_____

_____

_____

_____

Interpretation:

Date: _____   God Dream ☐   Soul Dream ☐

Emotion: _____

Category: _____

Focus(es): _____

Sub-focuses: _____

Dream: _____

_____

_____

_____

_____

_____

_____

_____

_____

_____

_____

_____

_____

_____

_____

_____

_____

_____

Interpretation:

Date: _____ God Dream ☐ Soul Dream ☐

Emotion: _____

Category: _____

Focus(es): _____

Sub-focuses: _____

Dream: _____

_____

_____

_____

_____

_____

_____

_____

_____

_____

_____

_____

_____

_____

_____

_____

_____

_____

Interpretation:

Date: _____ God Dream ☐   Soul Dream ☐

Emotion: _____

Category: _____

Focus(es): _____

Sub-focuses: _____

Dream: _____

_____

_____

_____

_____

_____

_____

_____

_____

_____

_____

_____

_____

_____

_____

_____

_____

_____

_____

_____

Interpretation:

Date: _____   God Dream ☐   Soul Dream ☐

Emotion: _____

Category: _____

Focus(es): _____

Sub-focuses: _____

Dream: _____

_____

_____

_____

_____

_____

_____

_____

_____

_____

_____

_____

_____

_____

_____

_____

_____

_____

_____

_____

Interpretation:

Date: _____ God Dream ☐   Soul Dream ☐

Emotion: _____

Category: _____

Focus(es): _____

Sub-focuses: _____

Dream: _____

_____

_____

_____

_____

_____

_____

_____

_____

_____

_____

_____

_____

_____

_____

_____

_____

_____

_____

Interpretation:

Date: _____   God Dream ☐   Soul Dream ☐

Emotion: _____

Category: _____

Focus(es): _____

Sub-focuses: _____

Dream: _____

_____

_____

_____

_____

_____

_____

_____

_____

_____

_____

_____

_____

_____

_____

_____

_____

Interpretation:

Date: _____ God Dream ☐ Soul Dream ☐

Emotion: _____

Category: _____

Focus(es): _____

Sub-focuses: _____

Dream: _____

_____

_____

_____

_____

_____

_____

_____

_____

_____

_____

_____

_____

_____

_____

_____

_____

_____

Interpretation:

Date: _____ God Dream ☐   Soul Dream ☐

Emotion: _____

Category: _____

Focus(es): _____

Sub-focuses: _____

Dream: _____

_____

_____

_____

_____

_____

_____

_____

_____

_____

_____

_____

_____

_____

_____

_____

_____

Interpretation:

Date: _____ God Dream ☐   Soul Dream ☐

Emotion: _____

Category: _____

Focus(es): _____

Sub-focuses: _____

Dream: _____

_____

_____

_____

_____

_____

_____

_____

_____

_____

_____

_____

_____

_____

_____

_____

_____

_____

Interpretation:

Date: _____ God Dream ☐   Soul Dream ☐

Emotion: _____

Category: _____

Focus(es): _____

Sub-focuses: _____

Dream: _____

_____

_____

_____

_____

_____

_____

_____

_____

_____

_____

_____

_____

_____

_____

_____

_____

_____

Interpretation:

Date: _____ God Dream ☐   Soul Dream ☐

Emotion: _____

Category: _____

Focus(es): _____

Sub-focuses: _____

Dream: _____

_____

_____

_____

_____

_____

_____

_____

_____

_____

_____

_____

_____

_____

_____

_____

_____

_____

Interpretation:

Date: _____ God Dream ☐   Soul Dream ☐

Emotion: _____

Category: _____

Focus(es): _____

Sub-focuses: _____

Dream: _____

_____

_____

_____

_____

_____

_____

_____

_____

_____

_____

_____

_____

_____

_____

_____

_____

_____

_____

_____

Interpretation:

Date: _____ God Dream ☐   Soul Dream ☐

Emotion: _____

Category: _____

Focus(es): _____

Sub-focuses: _____

Dream: _____

_____

_____

_____

_____

_____

_____

_____

_____

_____

_____

_____

_____

_____

_____

_____

_____

_____

Interpretation:

Date: _____ God Dream ☐   Soul Dream ☐

Emotion: _____

Category: _____

Focus(es): _____

Sub-focuses: _____

Dream: _____

_____

_____

_____

_____

_____

_____

_____

_____

_____

_____

_____

_____

_____

_____

_____

_____

_____

Interpretation:

Date: _____ God Dream ☐   Soul Dream ☐

Emotion: _____

Category: _____

Focus(es): _____

Sub-focuses: _____

Dream: _____

_____

_____

_____

_____

_____

_____

_____

_____

_____

_____

_____

_____

_____

_____

_____

_____

_____

Interpretation:

Date: _____ God Dream ☐   Soul Dream ☐

Emotion: _____

Category: _____

Focus(es): _____

Sub-focuses: _____

Dream: _____

_____

_____

_____

_____

_____

_____

_____

_____

_____

_____

_____

_____

_____

_____

_____

_____

_____

_____

_____

Interpretation:

Date: _____ God Dream ☐   Soul Dream ☐

Emotion: _____

Category: _____

Focus(es): _____

Sub-focuses: _____

Dream: _____

_____

_____

_____

_____

_____

_____

_____

_____

_____

_____

_____

_____

_____

_____

_____

_____

_____

Interpretation:

Date: _____ God Dream ☐   Soul Dream ☐

Emotion: _____

Category: _____

Focus(es): _____

Sub-focuses: _____

Dream: _____

_____

_____

_____

_____

_____

_____

_____

_____

_____

_____

_____

_____

_____

_____

_____

_____

_____

Interpretation:

Date: _____   God Dream ☐   Soul Dream ☐

Emotion: _____

Category: _____

Focus(es): _____

Sub-focuses: _____

Dream: _____

_____

_____

_____

_____

_____

_____

_____

_____

_____

_____

_____

_____

_____

_____

_____

_____

_____

Interpretation:

Date: _____ God Dream ☐ Soul Dream ☐

Emotion: _____

Category: _____

Focus(es): _____

Sub-focuses: _____

Dream: _____

_____

_____

_____

_____

_____

_____

_____

_____

_____

_____

_____

_____

_____

_____

_____

_____

_____

_____

_____

Interpretation:

Date: _____ God Dream ☐   Soul Dream ☐

Emotion: _____

Category: _____

Focus(es): _____

Sub-focuses: _____

Dream: _____

_____

_____

_____

_____

_____

_____

_____

_____

_____

_____

_____

_____

_____

_____

_____

_____

_____

Interpretation:

Date: _____ God Dream ☐   Soul Dream ☐

Emotion: _____

Category: _____

Focus(es): _____

Sub-focuses: _____

Dream: _____

_____

_____

_____

_____

_____

_____

_____

_____

_____

_____

_____

_____

_____

_____

_____

Interpretation:

Date: _____ God Dream ☐ Soul Dream ☐

Emotion: _____

Category: _____

Focus(es): _____

Sub-focuses: _____

Dream: _____

_____

_____

_____

_____

_____

_____

_____

_____

_____

_____

_____

_____

_____

_____

_____

_____

_____

_____

Interpretation:

Date: _____ God Dream ☐   Soul Dream ☐

Emotion: _____

Category: _____

Focus(es): _____

Sub-focuses: _____

Dream: _____

_____

_____

_____

_____

_____

_____

_____

_____

_____

_____

_____

_____

_____

_____

Interpretation:

About the Author

Amber N. Johnson MD is a physician, preacher, author, and international prophetic voice. She is the founder and president of *Arise Ministries* which has a mission to connect people to the heart of God and empower them to fulfill their Kingdom destinies. Amber ministers through online prophetic preaching, podcasts and classes to equip people in areas such as prophecy, deliverance, and dream interpretation. Amber often ministers in the realm of inner healing and deliverance, with a special emphasis on healing from past trauma. Through *Arise Ministries* she also equips developing leaders, with a vision to bring sustained revival to her city.

Arise Uganda Women's Ministry is a branch of *Arise Ministries* dedicated to widows and orphans in Uganda who are traditionally neglected and forced into homelessness. To love and empower these women, the ministry provides for physical, educational, spiritual, and social needs. The women are introduced to the love and truth of Jesus and empowered to learn trades to support themselves and their children. Amber has personally met most of the Ugandan ministers while in Uganda, and she continues to oversee, teach and lead the Ugandan ministry team virtually through online meetings.

Amber is also the founder of *Stand Fast in Freedom*, an organization established to provide healing and wholeness to trafficked youth in her home state of Nebraska. This ministry provides 24/7 residential care in an environment of love and hope. Through counseling, education and a family-type atmosphere, the girls are introduced to the healing love of Jesus and empowered to dream for the future.

Amber is the author of *You are Powerful: Embracing the Woman of Power and Purpose God Created You to Be*. She resides in Omaha, Nebraska.

To connect with Amber Johnson, visit:

www.ariseministries.life

www.ingramcontent.com/pod-product-compliance
Lightning Source LLC
Chambersburg PA
CBHW051211120626

46547CB00013B/1295

* 9 7 8 1 9 9 1 2 9 9 0 0 0 *